Overlooked

Rita B

My Why

*L*OOKING AT THE young girl in the picture, you never would have guessed that she was once broken, insecure, depressed, shy, lonely, undervalued, and felt unloved. I see why they say you should never judge a book by its cover.

My mom and I have a close bond, but I still couldn't tell her everything I went through growing up. I finally got the strength to tell her when I was thinking about writing this book. Young girls should feel comfortable talking to their parents or a trusted adult. Talking to someone is important.

So many young girls have gone through similar life experiences with no one to talk to. Throughout life, I felt isolated like I was this awful plague that people thought would rub off on them. My heart was full of anger and hurt. I wanted to be accepted just like everyone else. I didn't know that I was beautiful inside and out. Social media makes it easy to compare our lives to the next person, as comparison is the thief of joy.

After years of struggling, I finally gained the self-confidence I needed. Self-confidence is defined as a feeling of trust in one's abilities, qualities, and judgment. God made us all different. We need to know in our hearts that beauty is within.

The reason you see so many butterflies is because in my eyes they are one of God's most unique creations. Butterflies go through so many trails to turn into something so beautiful. The fact that scientists don't know how they evolve into the final stage to become a butterfly makes it more fascinating. I think about our lives and how we have to go through so much in life to become who we are today. The challenges of life turn us into the beautiful and strong ladies we are now.

I wrote this book because it took me years to love myself and I don't want another young girl waiting until adulthood to love the person that she sees every day. I know what it's like being teased and bullied. I longed to fit in, but it took me some time to realize that it was ok to be different. God didn't create me to fit in with everyone.

Each chapter includes lessons and tips in hopes to further educate you. Girls need to know that they are not alone. If this book can help at least one soul, then I have done my job because that one soul can change millions of lives.

Contents

Abandonment And It's Heartache 1

Silent Abuse 15

The Seed Of Insecurity Planted 23

The Voice That Saved My Life 33

Mind Battling 43

Be Aware Of Your Surroundings 49

Authentically You 55

The Beginning Of Something New 61

God's Protection 67

Betrayal 73

Looking For Love In All The Wrong Places 77

Loving The Skin You Are In 85

Never Let Your Past Hold You Down 89

There Is Beauty In Being Different 97

Don't Give Up On Life. Life's Good Outweighs The Bad ...101

Abandonment And It's Heartache

EW PEOPLE ARE fond of the Chicago projects. However, growing up in the Henry Horner projects on Chicago's Westside made me one of the few. There's something about hearing the trains on Lake Street and watching people sing and dance at the local talent shows that made it feel like home. They truly knew how to put on a show. I remember going to the Girls and Boys Club and hanging out with my friend Mariah. We would have so much fun that our stomachs would hurt from laughing so hard. The smell of mama's good cooking made me hungry as I played hopscotch on the 4th floor of the hallway where we stayed.

The Henry Horner projects may not have been the safest place to raise a child, but it was a community. Somehow, people always knew when something was about to happen. Word got around quickly, and the parents would tell all the children to get in the house. Later, we would find out that someone got shot.

The projects were home for me.

My earliest and fondest memory of my father is when he and I would walk to the corner store. This was my favorite thing to do with him because it was just him and me. He would let me get whatever I wanted and buy candy and snacks for my sisters. Some days when I would get tired of walking, he would pull me up on his shoulders and fly me around as if I was an airplane. He would make the sound of an airplane as I spread my wings and guided our path. Our laughter would fill the air. He would tell me how beautiful I was and how much he loved me. I was his precious jewel; his pride and joy. He always called me, "Lil Spot" because everyone called him, "Spot."

That memory would also be a painful one. One day, at the end of our walk, on the front stoop, he gave me a hug and a kiss and said goodbye. My father and my mom parted ways that day.

Unfortunately, I wouldn't see him for another two years. When I did, it was through a glass partition that was separating him from me and a telephone on each side that monitored our conversations. Over the time frame that my father was missing, he was in and out of jail because of his gang affiliations. My father would send me the prettiest letters that would warm my heart. He would tell me how much he loved and missed me. My father was a man in the streets that ran with the wrong crowd. That's probably the reason my mother and him broke up.

I would sit in my momma's lap, barely looking at my dad. I was never the talkative type so I would listen to him talk. I remember sadness. The entire place just felt sad. I would see women and other children crying when they were at the glass. It was heartbreaking. When it was time to go, my father would give me a big smile and say, "Daddy loves you Lil Spot." He would hold his hand to the glass and wait. Wait on me to press my hand against it. It was hard for me to put my hand up there. My mother would have to take my hand and put it against the glass for me.

Not being able to touch his hands or sit beside him was emotionally draining. I missed the walks and the airplane rides. I missed my dad.

My father wasn't able to come to any of my school activities or pack my lunch for me. My mom handled seeing me off to kindergarten every day with no help from my father. She dealt with the role of being a single parent to my sisters and me quite well. When she needed help, she could count on our grandmother and aunts to fill in where needed. She was a super mom because she made things happen. Our mom being there for our every need became the norm and so did seeing my father less and less.

My mom worked at the Boys and Girls Club. So as soon as we got out of school, we came straight to her. Between my grandmother and mother, they had a good routine going. It felt like a two-parent house because we didn't lack anything. I remember for my kindergarten graduation, my mother made the best dinner ever with all my favorites. There were no complaints from my sisters either. Everyone enjoyed dinner and had a good time that night.

I spent that summer hanging out with my grandmother, sisters, and cousins. I always had fun hanging out with them. They kept me laughing so much that I didn't realize that summer flew by so quick. Before you knew it, it was the first day of school. My mom dressed me and styled my hair with two ponytails with pink ribbons. She assured my face was not dry with all the Vaseline she put on me. I was smiling ear to ear because my mom made sure I looked my best.

First grade was ok, but it wasn't the same as kindergarten. Kindergarten I knew everyone, and we seemed to get along well. There were some new kids in the first-grade classroom, and they appeared as if they didn't like me. Not sure why. I tried sharing my toys and even helping them out in class, but it didn't help. It didn't bother me too much because I still knew most of my classmates and I got along with them well.

One particular Saturday, I was sitting on the porch with my grandmother on my father side, just enjoying the weather. I'm not sure where the thought I had came from but perhaps it was the perfect weather, and the idea of my father being here to enjoy it with me.

"Grandma, how's my daddy doing?" I asked.

"Well, I guess he is doing good up there in Wisconsin. He got himself a good job and doing pretty good for himself." She responded.

"Wisconsin?" I asked as I turned to look at her face to question her response. "What is my daddy doing in Wisconsin?"

The facial expression on my grandma's face led me to believe that it was information I wasn't supposed to know. I didn't even know my father was out of jail. *Why wouldn't they tell me?*

"Rita, I'm sorry I thought you knew your father was out. I'm sure he meant to tell you and meant nothing by it." Grandma said with a tone to soothe anyone with a broken heart.

"Ok. Grandma." I didn't bother to ask any more questions because the only word that came to mind was 'why?' Why didn't my father tell me? Why didn't my mother tell me? Why is he in Wisconsin? Why did he leave me? Why? 'Why' was all that mattered to me at the moment.

My mother was conveniently working late that day, so I wasn't able to ask her. Quite frankly, wasn't sure if I wanted to ask my mom. By the look on grandmother's face, I wasn't supposed to know. So 'why' continued to linger in the back of my head. Whenever I saw a young girl with her father, 'why' was right there to taunt me. Reminding me that my father decided to leave me and not even let me know.

It wasn't until the second- grade that I heard from my

father. I turned around at my desk in class and noticed a man standing in the doorway. I didn't recognize him at first. I sat there for about three seconds until I realized who he was.

I ran into the hallway, and he gave me the biggest hug and kiss and said he loved me.

"I missed you Lil Spot. Look what I have for you." He kneeled on one knee and in his hands was a gold Mickey Mouse necklace. It was beautiful. I smiled ear to ear as he placed the necklace around my neck. "Aww baby girl, that looks good on you!"

"Thank you, daddy," I said, but I wanted to cry out and tell him how much I missed him. How I wanted him home with me, but I didn't. I withheld my tears as I saw that a lady was standing afar looking at me and smiling.

I asked my dad if he knew the lady and he told me that she was a friend of his. I just looked puzzled but quickly dismissed it as my dad informed me that he was checking me out early for the day and took me to my grandmother's.

That day we- my grandmother, my father, his friend and I- talked at the kitchen table. It was at the kitchen table that my father told me he had moved to Wisconsin, unbeknownst to him my grandmother had previously spilled the beans. So, I continued as if I didn't already know. I asked him all about Wisconsin and what made him move. He explained that he had made trouble for himself down here and he wanted to be in a better environment. He wanted to become a better person, so he felt that moving was the best option.

"Daddy, why didn't you let me know you were out?" I asked trying to appease my curiosity.

"I didn't want to lose my life to the streets, so I had to focus on getting my life together." He said he wasn't thinking straight and apologized saying, "Sometimes the decisions we make in life, we don't understand how much it affects others. I promise I never meant to hurt you."

I smiled as his answer made me feel better. That day was short-lived as daddy got back on the road later on that evening. He told me he would call me so we could talk more. That promised lasted just as long as his visit.

The upcoming years weren't easy for me. Even though I knew where my father was, I felt abandoned. He was never around. I would watch kids get picked up by their fathers. I would watch them laugh and share those special moments, but not me. I wanted to hold his hand. I wanted his conversation.

As time passed, things got easier, but the pain was still there. I didn't hear from my father in years; no letters, no phone calls, no postcards, nothing. It was like I had become a forgotten memory. Time had passed, and I had given up on him. It was in fifth grade I learned that I had a little sister. I figured I wouldn't hear from him again because I was a part of his past and had been replaced. He had a new family to occupy his time, so you can only imagine the shock I had when he came down to visit me one summer with my little sister.

One morning the doorbell rang, and I sprint to the door thinking it was my friend. Not asking who it is, I open the door with a big smile. It was daddy standing there with his arms open wide.

"Lil Spot, come here and give daddy a hug." He said. I hugged him, but it was what was beside him that caught my attention. I noticed a woman standing beside him with a baby, the same woman that I saw at my school, that my dad introduced as a friend. My dad saw that my focus was on the lady standing beside him.

"Oh, Rita, you remember Ms. Jessica. This is Stacie's mother." Said my father to answer the lingering question in my head of *who is this lady "friend" that keeps showing up with my dad?*

"Nice to meet you again," I said.

"Would you like to hold her, Rita?" Ms. Jessica asked. "Would you like to hold your sister?"

As I nodded, my heart began to race. She was so small and fragile. Ms. Jessica weened Stacie off of her and placed her in my arms, making sure I supported the baby's head. She was gorgeous and smelled nice. It was something about babies I loved. My mother came outside, not surprised by my father's arrival, and gestured us to come in. We all went into the living room and talked. I got caught up on all of what daddy's been doing and his life with Ms. Jessica. She seemed ok, but in the back of my mind, I knew she was the reason my daddy didn't stay in contact with me. *No letters, nothing! I guess she occupies all his free time.* I didn't let it ruin the moment though. I was glad to know my daddy was ok and that my beautiful little sister was safe and sound. Surprisingly, my mom was nice to Ms. Jessica. I guess with daddy gone all this time, she's made her peace and had moved on. Mom was just as happy as I was. That summer was a great one. My daddy stayed in town, so I saw him more in two months than I did in three years. We were a makeshift happy family for those months. When the summer was over, it was hard to see him leave, but I was used to it by now.

A year and some months had gone by before I had another emotional episode about my father. I was over my grandmother's house when I saw pictures of him and Ms. Jessica's wedding. To make it worse, my grandmother was in some of them. My father got married and didn't even invite me. He only stayed two-and-a-half hours away. I approached my grandmother about the pictures.

"Grandma, my daddy got married and didn't tell me?" I asked. *How could he have a wedding and not invite me?* I thought.

"Aww baby, it was short notice. He didn't want to-" She tried to explain before I stormed off.

I didn't want to hear another excuse about my father. If he can't seem to call or write to me, then he didn't want me there. I'm over it and him. He can continue to live his happy life in Wisconsin as if I don't exist.

My heart was full of anger and rage towards my father. The same man who told me I was beautiful and special, treated me as if I was a 'has-been.'

In my seventh-grade year, my father and his wife were in town and stopped by. Mrs. Jessica was outside when I overheard her on the phone talking about me. She was telling someone that if it weren't for her, my dad wouldn't be in my life. She had to force my father to come and see me. After hearing that, I was done with him. *It wasn't her that was keeping him from me; it was him all along!* I avoided my father for the remainder of his stay.

It wasn't until I was in high school that I told my dad how mad I was with him. I wanted a father that would be there for me. I missed out on father-daughter dances and having a fatherly opinion. My father went ghost a lot of years of my life, and it hurt me. I shared all of how I felt.

He cried and apologized. He told me loved me, and it made me feel better. For me not to hurt anymore, I had to forgive my father. I understood now that he moved to save his life and to have a better future. But through it all, I didn't let that hurt determine my future. I would always ask myself why he left and God reminded me of Psalms 27: 10 'when my father and my mother forsake me, then the Lord will take me up.'

All those nights I cried, God was there. I've learned not to use my daddy issues as an excuse to act out. I have a strong mother that took the role as a mother and a father in my life that worked two jobs to provide for my sisters and me, quite well. We didn't have everything we wanted, but we had everything we needed. Some girls grow up without either. I realized that regardless of not having my father around that God still made a way for her to get everything done. Things may have gotten hard for her, but she didn't give up on us, and I appreciate her for everything she has done for us. But when you call on God, He will take you in and give the comfort that you need to go through hard times.

Over time, God took that rage and anger and turned it into understanding. I saw the situation from my father's eyes. I knew that he wasn't perfect and that he could've done better but he's human and we all make mistakes. After our heart to heart moment, our communication became regular. We still talk to this day more than ever. I love him unconditionally. I can talk to him about anything. I thought I would never have that type of relationship with him and I honor that. Here are six things you can do to forgive someone that has hurt you:

1. Remember that no one is perfect and we all fall short. We need to remember that even if someone has good intentions, they can still hurt you. We all make mistakes. Some mistakes are harder to recover from than others. People don't intentionally try to hurt others, and for those that do, they are in greater pain themselves. This helps you to see a person's humanity instead of seeing them in a negative light.

2. You have to want to forgive. I know it's hard, but for forgiveness to take place, it has to start with you wanting to forgive them. Holding onto the pain only hurts you more. It makes you feel justified for not forgiving them. No one can force you to forgive someone. Usually, anger and resentment are the reasons it's hard to forgive someone. We want them to hurt just as bad or even worse than we are hurting.

3. Realize that you can only control yourself and not others. See if there is anything you could learn from the situation. Perhaps I could've told my father earlier how his actions have hurt me instead of waiting years down the line. I'm not justifying my father's actions, just recognizing if there was anything I could've done to improve the situation.

4. If needed, talk to a trusted source about how you feel. Find someone that can pray with you and seek God with you regarding your healing. It may be hard to talk to the actual person who has hurt you because you are so angry and you feel as if you can explode; so practice what you would say to the person with a trusted source. They should understand that you're not attacking them, just working out some of your issues. If you still don't feel comfortable talking to someone, try practicing in the mirror.

5. When you forgive, let it go, and don't pick it back up. The purpose of forgiving is to heal and move on. It's harder to recover from hurt when you're

thinking about it every five minutes. Don't bring back up the hurt to the person you have forgiven, either. People have the tendency to bring the past, to win arguments or to make the other person feel bad.

6. Take time for yourself. If someone has wronged you, taking time apart can help. It will allow you to go through your thoughts and feelings and even gain perspective on the situation. Sometimes being a parent is hard. They don't always have the answers, but they do the best they can with what they have. As I am a parent now, I see the struggle my mother and father went through. I encourage you to pray for your parents and when you do, keep Exodos 20:12 in mind "Honor your father and your mother, so you may live long in the land the Lord your God is giving you." Here's a prayer that you can say to help you.

FATHER GOD,

I thank You for the gift of forgiveness that brings healing and reconciliation. Even though I may be angry, resentful or scared, my emotions don't have control over me. Colossians 3:13 says, "make allowance for each other's faults, and forgive anyone who offends you. Remember, the Lord forgave you, so you must forgive others." Jesus, You have forgiven us of our sins so, Lord, help me to forgive those who have hurt me, intentional or not. Lord, help me to take any ungodly thoughts captive and make them obedient to Christ.

Let Your spirit of peace fill my heart and allow me to love them the same way that You love them. We are all Your children, and You love us the same. Thank You for honoring my prayer according to God's will. In Jesus mighty name, I pray. Amen.

Silent Abuse

THEY SAY IT takes a village to raise a child. Ms. Williams, unfortunately, was a part of that village. Ms. Williams was a good friend of my daddy side of the family that built a close relationship with my mother. Before my daddy was in and out of jail, Ms. Williams was dating a friend of my fathers. Her and my mom hit it off. Their bond grew closer over time. Ms. Williams was a stout woman who commanded attention when walking into a room. It wasn't because of her beauty but more so her demeanor. She had a smile that seemed more awkward than pleasant. She seemed deceivingly nice.

Her children were around the same age as me, so when she and my mother would get together, my sisters and I would play with them. They seemed really cool but somewhat timid if they were having too much fun. Couldn't explain it but thought it was weird. I didn't too much care to figure it out because I was just happy to have someone else to play with besides my sisters.

One day my mother and Ms. Williams were sitting down at the kitchen table talking and catching up while her kids and I were watching television.

"Rita, come here." My mom yells.

"Coming," I yelled back assuring her I was coming as I took my time getting up because I didn't want to miss the best part of the show.

"Rita!"

"Yes, ma'am," I said as I made haste to the kitchen. Upon entering my mother and Ms. Williams were laughing and didn't even notice my presence in the kitchen. It wasn't until I cleared my throat that someone acknowledged me.

"Oh, I'm sorry Rita. Ms. Williams's wants to know how you would feel if you spent the night over her house? You can spend some time playing with the kids, and you won't be cooped up in the house all day with your sisters." She asked.

"Cool. Thanks, mom!" I hurried off back into the other room to tell the kids I would be hanging out with them over the weekend. They were excited to have me over. We made plans to stay up all night playing games. They were determined that I would be the first one to fall asleep. I assured them it would not be me.

Later that day when it was time to go, I was so excited. We all piled in Ms. Williams car and played as if we weren't going to be with each other for the weekend.

"Listen here. I know y'all like to have fun and all, but I'm not up for all that noise in my house. Steve,

Theresa and Jasmine, y'all know what the deal is." Says Ms. Williams as her voice shifts the atmosphere of the car and breaks our mood. We sat quietly in the back seat looking straight ahead. I looked at the kids, and they were sitting like statues. So, I sat still.

Wasn't too much of a ride left after Ms. Williams interrupted our fun. I was ready to get out of the car.

When we arrived at her house, we rushed into the bedroom and played again. We were sure to be quiet; we thought. About twenty minutes into us playing, Ms. Williams comes in abruptly.

"What did I tell you all?" She asks with no intention of us responding as she popped all us on our mouths and told us to get ready for bed. We changed our clothes and laid down. In the spirit of us not wanting to go to bed and not able to talk, that night we came up with our own language. A combination of hand movements and silly faces is how we communicated. We made stuff up as we were going and half the time we forgot what we had come up with, but we had fun.

We stayed up as late as we could, and I wasn't the first to go to bed.

The next morning, Ms. Williams awakened us with a loud bang on the door.

"Breakfast ready," she says just as loud as her bang on the door. "And don't take forever to get up either. I have some errands to run."

We got up promptly without hearing any more lip from Ms. Williams. Ms. Williams's breakfast wasn't so bad, but it wasn't as good as my mom's though. After breakfast, she told us to take showers, brush our teeth and get ready. Since I was the guest, they allowed me to go first. Ms. Williams assured me that there was a five-minute limit on showers, so I better hit all the important places. I nodded assuring her I wouldn't be over five minutes.

I saw a side of Ms. Williams that I didn't see when my mother was around. I guess it's because the children aren't allowed in grown folks conversation, because all I ever saw was her and mom talking for hours.

I took my shower, got dressed and waited for the others. Ms. Williams told me to come into the living room so she could do my hair.

"Keep your head still." She said moving my head back in a particular angle as she braided my hair.

"Ooouuuchhh." I yelped as she popped me with the comb.

"What did I tell you? Keep your head still or you gonna have another one coming."

I dare not respond to her that my head *was* still. I sat there hoping she would finish soon without popping me again.

Once we were all ready, we loaded up into the car. Ms. Williams informed us that she had to make a few stops and we need to be on our best behavior.

"Yes, ma'am." We all said in unison.

We continued to play in the back seat, building

upon the language we created last night. We pulled up to our first stop and hopped out. Ms. Williams was walking at a fast pace. We were not too far behind when she turned around and hit me.

"Keep up. I don't have time to lose no children." She addressed us all even though I was the one she hit. I'm not sure if she thought I was one of her own, but she kept walking without missing a beat. I was starting not to like Ms. Williams. I remained in front of her from then on. When we got into the store, the items on the shelves fascinated us. Before we could lay a finger on it, Ms. Williams, popped Theresa and me.

"Do y'all have any money to buy anything? - Well then, I suggest you not touch anything! Next person to touch something, is gonna get my belt!"

Theresa flinched at her mom's quick reflexes, while I stood there with my mouth poked out. I didn't get hit this much with my mamma! Theresa looked at me with such sympathy as to say, please be my friend still.

The rest of the errands, we were sure to stay up front, keep quiet and touch nothing. We made it back to the house with no one getting popped until Steve accidentally dropped a bag of groceries which broke some eggs. When we got into the house, he got the belt. I was so ready to go home. I didn't want to be next in line for the belt.

That night I wasn't in much of a playing mood. I suggested that we watch a movie and eat some popcorn that we got from the store. I didn't care if I was the first to go to bed; I just wanted to be back home.

The next day on the way home before I got out of the car, Ms. Williams made it clear that what happened at her house stays at her house. I was glad to have left her care. I dashed into the house before she could get out.

"Woo, woo. Slow down, young lady. How was your weekend?" My mom asked stopping me midway to my room.

"Good," I said as Ms. Williams interrupted me coming through the front door.

"Hello? Where is everyone?" Asked Ms. Williams.

"Coming. I'll meet you in the kitchen, Linda." My mom responded.

My mom patted me on the head and left me to meet Ms. Williams in the kitchen.

"So, was she on her best behavior Linda?" My mom asked.

"Oh, yes. She was an angel. No, bother at all." Ms. Williams responded.

I heard them make small talk and laugh for a minute before Ms. Williams left. I went into my room and chilled for the rest of the day with my sisters.

That weekend wasn't the last weekend of me dealing with Ms. Williams. She would watch me from time to time and eventually over time I became like Theresa, flinching every time I thought she would hit me. One day she wanted to take me to the store, and I remember her hitting me so hard that I started crying. People were looking, and I was wondering why no one helped me. She always wanted to spend time with me knowing what she used to do to me and I never understood why.

Ms. Williams used to pinch and punch me so hard I started seeing purple bruises. I hid the bruises so my mom wouldn't be hurt or upset. I didn't want to be a bother to her. Not knowing that if I would've told my mom, she would've saved me.

Most people are familiar with physical abuse as it leaves signs such as marks, scratches, black eyes, etc. No one has the right to intentionally harm you, even if it is an adult. However, physical abuse isn't the only type of abuse. No one should place you in harm's way, neglect your needs (such as food, clothing or shelter), make you feel undeserving or less than, expose you to inappropriate activities such as drugs, sex or alcohol.

If anyone of these things is happening to you, please speak up to an adult you trust. If you want to learn about some myths and facts about child abuse, please go to Helpguide.com. Don't ever think you would be a burden on a person for telling them your problems. It could've been stopped, but I was too afraid to say anything.

Abuse is a sensitive topic and can be challenging to deal with. If you are dealing with abuse, please get the help you need. If you are within the United States or Canada and experiences abuse, call Childhelp at

1-800-422-4453 or visit Child Welfare Information Gateway. If you are being abused, please seek professional help. Here is a prayer you can say to help you during your time of need.

FATHER GOD,

I plead the blood of Jesus over my life, my body, my spirit and against anyone who means me harm. I ask for Your divine protection. Comfort my heart, heal my wounds, and transform me from a place of brokenness to a place of being whole. May Your perfect love drive out fear and anxiety. Lord, help me to forgive those that have done me wrong. They were not operating under the love of God, and I pray for their deliverance. Allow them to be filled with Your love and grace. We asked that Your name is glorified in this situation. In Jesus mighty name. Amen.

The Seed Of Insecurity Planted

MY MOTHER WAS a single parent of three girls working hard to make ends meet. Even with her busy schedule, she was there when we needed her. She loved us. We were her pride and joy. Throughout second and third grade, she would dress us alike, clothes and hairstyles. However, the oldest sister could wear a different hairstyle from us.

We stayed in a two-bedroom apartment. My sister's and I shared a room. My oldest sister had a bed to herself while the middle sister and I shared a bed. You could imagine that it wasn't easy sharing a room and a bathroom with my sisters.

My mom was an attractive fair-skinned woman, beautiful hair and a smile that brightened your day. My sisters and I all had different fathers, and our mother treated us equally. Even though my mother loved us the same, my sisters treated me differently.

The first time my sisters treated me different was when they informed me that I was adopted. I didn't know what being adopted meant. By the look on my face, they knew I didn't know the meaning, and they ran away laughing. I didn't think much of it as we went back to playing. Later, I asked my mom if she adopted me and she got mad. My mom assured me I wasn't.

When my oldest sister was of age to babysit us, that's when things got worse for me. At night, my sisters would tell me to come into the kitchen with them to get a snack. They would push me down on the floor and turn off all the lights. They would run to the bedroom, bang on the door and call my name to scare me. They would tell me I was too black to be their sister. They made up songs, walking to school, singing about how black I was. They even said that our mother put me in the oven, and I got burnt, so that's why I was darker than them. Not to mention that my birthmark was light so they would say that was a spot that our mother missed.

I would run into a corner crying, furious at my sisters, wondering if I wasn't their sister. To make it worst I was already being teased in school. Through second and third grade I was mostly with my friend Mariah. Mariah was easy to talk to and someone that understood me. She didn't judge me off of my looks. She actually got to know me, and because of that, we became good friends.

Unlike Mariah, the other kids still teased me, not wanting to be around me. I didn't understand why I was so 'bad' to be around. I thought spending my allowance money on candy would make the other kids like me. It worked until the candy ran out, then they started back teasing me.

My sisters were fair skinned like our mother. Both of their first names began with an M, and both of their last names started with an A. My first name began with an L, and my last name started with a B. The more I thought about what they were saying, the more it bothered me. My sisters would tease me all the time. *Maybe I was too black to be their sister?* I would always ponder about it until one day I ask my mother why was I darker than my sisters, and she said that my father has a darker skin complexion and that's why I'm the beautiful color I am.

When I was eight years old, I was at the park with my cousins and sisters. My mother allowed me to bring my doll. As I was playing with her, an older cousin snatched the doll from me. She told me the doll was to light for me and I should have gotten a burnt doll to match my skin complexion. She ran around the park, tossing the doll back and forth to my other cousin, throwing it in the dirt. She kept yelling that she was trying to match my doll's skin complexion with mine by rubbing her face in the mud. I tried to chase her, but she was too fast. I cried, but that didn't help either. No one would give me my doll back. They destroyed her.

I left the park, drying my tears, heading straight home to tell my mother how they were treating me. My grandmother, on my mother's side of the family, drove school buses for a living. She was sitting in front of my house, on her school bus and saw me walking pass. She could tell that something was wrong with me.

"Rita," She called out. "My beautiful child come here and tell grandma what's the matter."

I shook my head too ashamed to speak with tears forming in my eyes. I didn't look at her because if I looked into her eyes, a flood of tears would have rushed out.

"You know you can't let what people say bother you. Tell them sticks and stones may break my bones, but words will never hurt me." She said in her loving voice.

"Yes, grandma. I know." I nodded my head and wiped away the one tear that escaped. It seemed like the ones you love the most hurt you the greatest. I never made it upstairs to tell my mother. I stayed on the bus that day with my grandmother. She made me laugh and forget all about the doll. I loved that she could make me laugh and turned playing on the school bus into an adventure. From her silly faces to funny jokes, I enjoyed every moment with her.

Bullies are everywhere. Bullying doesn't just happen from strangers; it can be from a loved one. Bullying can be physical, psychological, verbal, or even over the Internet and social media. Being bullied by family can mentally and emotionally scar you as you assume they have your best interest in mind.

Realize, regardless of the person, people bully others,

to make themselves feel better. Family members hurt too and even misdirect their feelings onto others. This behavior is not acceptable but it happens.

The cruelty I experienced from my family is inexcusable, and it hurt, but beyond that, I forgave them. Ephesians 4:32 (ESV) tells us to be kind to one another, tenderhearted, forgiving one another, as God in Christ forgave you. It may be hard to forgive those that hurt you, but you must do it. Luke 17:3-4 states "Take heed to yourselves: If thy brother trespass against thee, rebuke him, and if he repents, forgive him. And if he trespasses, against thee seven times in a day, and seven times in a day turn again to thee, saying, I repent; thou shalt forgive him."

Forgiving someone isn't for them; it's for you. It's saying that your feelings no longer bind you and that you're willing to move forward. You will no longer be bound by what happened in the past. The adverse mental effects of bullying can be long term. I forgave them because I didn't want to stay in the past. I got tired of reliving that hurt as an adult.

Forgiveness can be a process for some, but in the meantime, I want to provide practical tips you can use to help stop the bullying, whether or not it's from a family member:

1. Tell a trusted adult. I never told my mom because I knew as a single mom, she was doing her best. I didn't want to bother her. We have to learn how to speak up for ourselves. Don't be shy or afraid to

do so. Someone needs to know so you can get the proper help.

2. Stand up for yourself and tell them to stop. It may be hard to do, but bullies rarely expect someone to stand up to them. They often target kids they believe they can intimidate. Take a stance for yourself and tell them to stop. Be confident in doing so. Stand tall and look them in the eye. No matter the result you would have gained confidence by speaking up for yourself.

3. Make a joke or even agree with the bully. This may sound strange, but if you have a sense of humor, you may make the bully defenseless by showing them you are confident in who you are, and their tactics don't work on you.

4. Avoid where they hang out. This is harder to do if the bully is a sibling or if you have a class together but if you can avoid where a bully hangs out, by all means, do so. Sometimes it's as simple as avoiding them to avoid being bullied.

5. This one may be a stretch but pray for your bully. Pray for the love of God to capture their heart and ease any anger, frustration, hurt or bitterness that may have caused them to bully you.

Bullying can have a lasting effect but know it's not your fault. Don't blame yourself. The only way to begin the healing process is to recognize that the bullying occurred and that you were not responsible for it. If you are experiencing issues such as anxiety, stress, insomnia, feelings of loneliness and isolation or suicidal thoughts, please seek professional help. Speak to a school counselor, parents or a trusted adult. You don't have to go through it alone.

I have provided a prayer below. As you pray, remember Mark 11: 22-25 which states, "Have faith in God, Jesus answered. Truly I tell you, if anyone says to this mountain, Go, throw yourself into the sea, and does not doubt in their heart but believes that what they say will happen, it will be done for them. Therefore, I tell you, whatever you ask for in prayer, believe that you have received it, and it will be yours. And when you stand praying, if you hold anything against anyone, forgive them, so that your Father in heaven may forgive you your sins."

You have to believe in what you are praying for!

HEAVENLY FATHER,

I thank You for the opportunity to come before You. Lord, You are my rock, my fortress, my strong tower. Thank You for being my refuge of safety from those who are trying to hurt me. Thank You for being my Savior who never leaves me or abandons me. I declare that Your angels will protect me wherever I go and that no hurt, harm or danger shall come near me. I thank You, God, for Your divine protection. I thank You, God, that You have all power and can change the heart of a bully. Father, forgive people who bully others. Lord, remind all of us of those we need to forgive; and help us be quick to forgive. Forgive me for not always speaking up and telling an adult when bullying is happening. Lord, help me find the strength to speak up against my bully. Give me courage like David to stand up to my Goliath. I pray that You touch the heart of the bully Lord. I pray that You mend whatever is broken and heal all their hurt. God, I pray they feel Your love as You chisel away from their hardened heart. I pray that You give them a heart of humility, love, and respect for others. In Jesus mighty name, I pray. Amen.

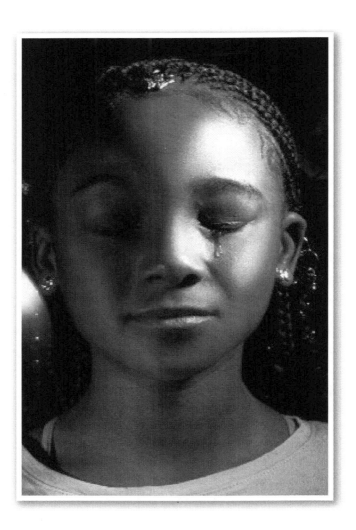

The Voice That Saved My Life

*I*N FOURTH GRADE, my mom moved us from the projects into a nice place. I was nervous that I had to meet all new people, but on the first day of school, I met Ashley. We clicked and were inseparable. You could find us laughing in the hallways, passing notes in class and talking about any and everything. Ashley made fourth grade fly by so smooth.

Fifth grade, I tried to make friends, but I got teased a lot by the other kids. One of the main things they teased me about was my flat chest. All the other girls were developing at that time, and I wasn't. I didn't like being me because no one else liked me. I had my one loyal friend though, Ashley. I was excited that it was my last year of elementary school. I was looking forward to a fresh start in middle school, hoping to put all the hurt behind me.

The school year went, as usual, people making jokes

about me because I didn't do what everyone else did. It didn't hurt as much, but it still made me cry. It was like every year it got worse. Why would people be so mean?

On Friday, my best friend and I were discussing our plans for the weekend. We were walking down the hallway minding our business when a classmate yelled 'she's a bust down.' I searched around not sure who he was referring to, but I discovered it was me. Everybody in the hallway stared at me in disgust and laughed. Girls were turning up their nose and rolling their eyes at me. I didn't even know what a 'bust down' was. The mere fact of people laughing at me caused me to retreat to the girl's bathroom. Ashley followed.

I ran right into a stall as if I was superman changing outfits ready to fly away. I wish!

"Rita, come out! Don't listen to those boys. They don't know what they're talking about." She pleaded with me.

"No! The whole school is laughing at me. I wish I could go home. I don't even know what a 'bust down' is."

"Well, I do, and you're not one. Rita, come out. There's no one in here. Please."

As a precaution, I opened the door an inch at a time just in case someone came in. I wiped my tears away with the sleeves of my shirt. Ashley got me some tissue out of the stall so I could blow my nose. The bell had rung signifying that class was in session. She allowed me to cry on her shoulder until I calmed down.

"What is a bust down?" I asked.

"You don't want to know."

"I do want to know. I want to know what they are calling me." I insisted.

"Well, it's a girl that- You know." She made gestures with her hand.

"A girl that what?" I said sounding frustrated.

"A girl that goes down on a guy."

"Eewww. What? *Why would he say that? I didn't do that! I don't even know him!*" I yelled.

Knowing what 'bust down' meant made me cry all over again.

"Nooooo. Stop that. See that's why I didn't want to tell you. You're not a bust down Rita. Those boys are stupid and have nothing else better to do. I know you wouldn't do anything like that." She said.

"I know you know, but the whole school thinks I do! I'm tired of everybody."

Another 15 minutes had passed by before I calmed down again and left the bathroom. I walked down the hallway with so much shame. As I entered the classroom, the teacher looked at me with a stern look. The class laughed, and her stern look turned into a look of sympathy as she pointed me to my seat.

That was the longest fifteen minutes of my life. I couldn't focus on anything my teacher was saying. I kept replaying the incident over in my mind. Why did he say that about me? Maybe he got the wrong person. Who would do that? Those were all the thoughts running through my head. It was now time for lunch. No one sat with me; everyone avoided me as if I was a plague besides Ashley.

I was so glad when it was time to go home. When the dismissal bell rang, I grabbed my stuff, and I ran home and closed myself in the room. My sisters were busy outside playing, so no one bothered me, nor did I care to speak about the incident. I cried myself to sleep and didn't bother to eat dinner either.

The next morning, I woke up to the smell of bacon, pancakes, and eggs. Momma was throwing down in the kitchen. My sisters were in the living room watching cartoons by the time I woke up. Momma called us to the dinner table, and we all ate breakfast together. I wasn't in the most talkative mood, so I ate quickly.

After we finished eating breakfast, I asked if I could go to the park to play with Mya, a friend from the neighborhood. She told me I had to shower first and wait another hour just in case her parents weren't up.

I did as my mother told me. I walked to Mya's house, and she came out. We walked to the park. Mya loved sports. There were some other girls there on the court that were friends with Mya. We walked over there to sit down with them. The other girls looked at me as if I was a foreign object they had never seen before. They pulled Mya aside and whispered something in her ear. I couldn't hear what they said, but Mya looked as if she didn't care, said ok and walked back to me. Mya suggested for us to do something else and I agreed, but I asked Mya what they said.

"They told me they couldn't hang with me when I'm with you. They said that you had a bad reputation and they don't want to be seen with you." She admitted. I admired Mya because she was confident in who she was and didn't try to appease anyone.

When she told me I was shocked. The thought that they didn't get to know me or even asked if the rumors were true bothered me. They just judged me based on what everyone else said. They looked at me in disgust as we walked away.

We left the park, and I made up an excuse to go home because I was so hurt. I closed the door to my bedroom and cried. My tears had soaked my pillow. I felt as if there was no hope for me. People would never accept me for who I am. So many thoughts came to mind. I felt worthless as if things wouldn't get better. *Why was it hard to fit in and have friends?*

I had an idea and managed to make it to my mother's washroom undetected. I went into my mother's cabinet and got her pills. I thought about getting a knife to cut myself or even hang myself, but I couldn't stomach the idea and thought pills were much easier. There were so many thoughts running through my mind. I just wanted the pain to leave. I felt as if I was losing it. My voice wasn't the only voice I was hearing. I heard a voice tell me not to do it and that it will be ok. Just live to see another day. Another voice said to me that no one loved me so I would be doing everyone a favor. I was toiling with these voices in my head, and after some time, I listened to the stronger voice. I didn't want my life to end; I just wanted the hurt to stop. I thought suicide would end all of my problems, but deep down I knew it would be selfish of me to end my life knowing my family love me. It wouldn't have solved anything it would have only made things worse.

After that night I knew someone was looking after me. It was the voice that saved my life. That night I had a strong desire to get to know God. I wanted to know more about Him. I would go to my grandmother's house on my father side, occasionally. We would sit and eat raisins. I would a talk to her about God. She was full of wisdom, but sometimes it would be too deep for my understanding. So, I reached out to my oldest sister to see if she could take me to church. She attended Chicago State University which wasn't far from home. She would let me spend some weekends with her in the dorms when she was free. I enjoyed spending time with her and learning more about God with her. She made it easy for me to understand.

It was fifteen years later that I found out why my classmate yelled that about me. He found me on social media and apologized. I was very reluctant to communicate with him but after on his third attempt of saying hello, he started off by saying 'I'm sorry.' He explained that his cousin had walked him to school that morning, and all the boys were talking about their encounters with girls. The cousin pointed me out. So later on, in the day when my classmate saw me walking down the hallway, he thought it would be funny to yell that out. It spread like wildfire, and everyone believed it. He said he was joking as we were all kids and didn't know any better. What he thought was funny, broke me. His joke nearly made me end my life but thank God it didn't.

Proverbs 18:21 (NIV) states "The tongue has the power of life and death, and those who love it will eat its fruit." Psalm 141:3 also states "Set a guard over my mouth, LORD; keep watch over the door of my lips." You need to understand that your words' impact people. That impact can be good or bad. So be mindful of the words you speak. Unlike the nursery rhyme of 'sticks and stones may break my bones and words will never hurt me,' words hurt as they have power.

The enemy will use anyone and anything to discourage you and keep you away from your greatness. Stand firm in the Word of God and know that you are fearfully and wonderfully made. Know your worth on the inside, even when people don't see your value on the outside.

We are a chosen people, a royal priesthood, a holy nation, God's special possession. God called you out of darkness into His marvelous light, 1 Peter 2:9 (NIV). When people talk about you and lie on you, know you are of royalty. God chose you. You are special to Him and made in His image. Know every tear you've shed; He is mindful of you. Your life is valuable. You are precious and let no one or anything tell you otherwise.

Did you know even Jesus had someone close to him betray him? Mark 14:10 (ISV) tells us "Then Judas

Iscariot, one of His twelve disciples, went to the high priests to betray Jesus to them." Don't feel as if you are going through your situation alone. Jesus knows what you are going through and He can give you the strength you need to get through it. If you have any thoughts of hurting yourself reach out to someone you can trust. Endure to the end. Even Jesus went through long-suffering. He didn't give up on us. So, don't give up on yourself. Pray for peace during your storm and also the strength to overcome it.

Here are three things you can do to handle people who talk bad about you;

1. Foremost, don't hate them. Don't let their hate turn you into a hater. Forgive them and pray for them. It's easier said than done. The enemy wants you to become bitter and mean just like them but don't allow it. You can stop it by showing them love. Many times people are mean to others because they have issues with themselves. Perhaps what they hate about you could be the one thing they hate about themselves, or what they hate about you is really what they secretly admire about you. So, when they have a problem with you, don't take it personally.

2. Make it right. Instead of assuming the worse and wondering, address your hater head-on, lovingly and kindly. If you need an adult present, please get one. Let them know what they have done and how it has made you feel. It's a possibility they didn't even know they were coming off in that manner.

3. Ignore them. Some people enjoy being mean, resentful and bitter. No matter what you do, they will continue to be mean. Just ignore them and know it's not you. It's them. You did nothing to them to deserve the treatment you are receiving. Just remember, you tried to make it right before you ignored them.

Below is a prayer on how to handle people that don't like you. As you pray, remember Luke 6:27-28 (ESV), "But I say to you who hear, love your enemies, do good to those who hate you, bless those who curse you, pray for those who abuse you."

DEAR GOD,

You are a God who values unity and peace, not quarreling and strife. God, when someone speaks to me in an ugly manner, let my words be full of grace. Let me not be full of anger and rage but of love and compassion for them. Let me not be bothered by their pettiness but be mature enough to pray for them. I pray that they begin to love themselves more. I pray that they allow the love of God to enter into their hearts. God help me to be strong in the face of my enemies. Don't let me repay evil with evil but give me a heart bold enough to love my enemy and even bless them (1 Peter 3:9). Allow me to identify the hurts and issues in their lives and how I can be of help to them. Please clear my heart of any issues that will hinder me from praying for those around me. In Jesus mighty name I pray. Amen.

Mind Battling

WE'VE ALL SEEN in films, the righteous and the evil angels on a person's shoulder telling them what they should do during a crucial decision. While both sides make persuasive points, in the end, it is ultimately up to that person to make the decision and determine the kind of person they want to be or what to do. Angels on our shoulders is a visual representation for the voices we hear in our minds. Some may call it their conscious while others believe it to be the voices of holy and fallen angels. These voices will contradict one another and leave you to make the decision. Sometimes you may hear one voice, and it is not the holy angel. If you hear voices telling you to harm yourself or someone else, it is not a voice of reason or righteousness. Those evil thoughts that come into your head want you to do evil and pursue their work. Just like how God wishes to spread good, faith, and kindness. Evil wants you to spread hate, fear, and darkness.

As a young girl with dark skin and different features from my peers, I was the target of bullying. I felt isolated and hopeless. I heard voices telling me to kill myself because it would make the pain go away. At the same time, I heard a voice telling me that everything would be okay and to stay strong.

If you feel like the dark and evil voices are overwhelming, you have to know that you are in charge of your thoughts and actions. Combat those negative thoughts with positive thoughts.

Regardless of how a person treats you, continue to have a good heart. Don't change being good for no one.

You are strong enough to ignore the voices by surrounding yourself with positive energy through friendship, family, and prayer. Call on God, and He will listen to your prayers. Praying to God doesn't always need to be at a church or in a church setting. You can pray at the foot of your bed, in the car, at a sports game, etc. But, remember to pray when you need to tell God about your doubts, pain, thoughts, or just to talk about your day.

There would be times that I would be asleep, and I couldn't move. The enemy would attack me in my sleep and bind my mouth. I couldn't pray. All I could do was call on the name of Jesus in my mind. As I continuously called on Jesus in my mind, I could feel the presence of God coming over me. I could feel the enemy's grip being released. Eventually, I would be able to speak the name of Jesus out of my mouth, and I would be free.

Even when you can't pray or know what to say, there is so much power in the name of Jesus. Before I go to bed now, I play gospel music and pray to ensure that God's presence is in my home. This helps me out tremendously, so I no longer get attacked.

The enemy does those things to try to put fear in us. I also believe that God let certain things happen in life to help us overcome these obstacles to make us stronger. Pray against fear and always take heed in knowing that God has not given us the spirit of fear, but of power, love, and of a sound mind as it states in 2 Timothy 1:7. When you feel as if fear is trying to creep in pull out your bible and read scriptures on fear and pray. Always remember John 4:18 "There is no fear in love. But perfect love drives out fear because fear has to do with punishment. The one who fears is not made perfect in love."

Always pray because you have a purpose in this world even if the reason seems small. But, do not confuse easy for right and good for evil. As stated in the book of Isaiah, "Woe to those who call evil good and good evil, who put darkness for light and light for darkness, who put bitter for sweet and sweet for bitter (Isa 5:20 ESV)!" Evil knows your weaknesses and how to use them to their advantage by giving you free passes. For example, if you forgot to study for a test and a friend next to you offers you a look at their test while taking it, this is a form of temptation. It's easy to pass the test by taking your friend's offer and cheating, but God sees all and knows that you've allowed evil to persuade your judgment. It might not be your fault that evil has presented itself, but it's only you at fault if you accept the offer. Once evil knows you go for easy alternatives, it will keep feeding you and presenting these alternatives to you until darkness consumes you.

When I was in a state of darkness and needed to tell someone about what battle was going on inside my head, I heard a voice telling me not to tell anyone. It would say that if I told anyone, it would make things worse. However, keeping deep, dark emotions and thoughts bottled inside is not good. If you're not ready to talk to a trusted adult like your parents, a guidance counselor, or a teacher, then write what you're feeling in a journal. Putting your emotions and thoughts onto a page is like casting away one evil spell after another. It lightens your mind, heart, and spirit. When you write in a journal, you're also talking to God in a way that no else can hear or understand. You can even address the passage to God in your journal if that's how you wish to communicate with Him. However, if you've been writing in a journal and notice the negative thoughts aren't going away or the passages are getting darker, then you need to seek help from someone who may understand what you're going through. A great person in your school setting to turn to is your guidance counselors. They are there for more than just creating your schedule. They are perhaps certified psychologists. This means they have lots of training on people who need help mentally with their thoughts and emotions.

Never think that you're doing something wrong.

Everything will be okay no matter how dark the world around you may seem. God is always with you. He said He would never leave you nor forsake you. Just know that you can overcome any and everything with Christ by your side. When evil thoughts come to your head, out of the blue, start praying against it. Surround yourself with positivity like affirmation posters in your room, uplifting and feel good books, movies with happy endings, and friends to always count on when you need an open mind and an open heart. Evil will always try to tempt you with free passes because it sees your potential and willingness to leave the darkness behind. I've been told that with every greater level is a bigger devil. But when you realize that God is in control over everything, you will know that you have already won the battle with Christ by your side. Even with the smallest issues in my life, I knew that God was holding my hand. Sometimes we worry about the littlest things when in reality we need to let go and stand firm on God's words. Evil presents itself every opportunity. By keeping God in your heart and acknowledging him daily, that will keep you out of the darkness and truly lead you to a blessed life.

One lesson that I learned when it comes to controlling your mind is to pray. When you pray, back every word up with scripture, trust and believe God is going to come through. The enemy tries to plant a seed in us, and it's up to us if we let it manifest. Change your thoughts through prayer and positivity. Below are a couple of verses to help you whenever the enemy tries to control your thoughts.

Philippians 4:8 (ESV), "Finally, brothers, whatever is true, whatever is honorable, whatever is just, whatever is pure, whatever is lovely, whatever is commendable, if there is any excellence, if there is anything worthy of praise, think about these things."

Also, Romans 12:2 (ESV), "Do not be conformed to this world, but be transformed by the renewal of your mind, that by testing you may discern what the will of God is, what is good and acceptable and perfect."

HEAVENLY FATHER,

When I am overwhelmed with stress and anxiety, help me to calm my mind and remember who You are in my life. When the enemy comes to tempt me and led me astray help me to remember James 4:7 that I should submit myself unto You and to resist the devil and he shall flee. Help me to continue to trust in You and Your word because according to Numbers 23:19, You are not a man that should lie, so I know Your word is true by faith. God, thank You for being faithful to me even when I am not faithful to You. Lord, thank You for continuing to protect me. Lord, I give You the authority over my life, my mind, my body, and soul. I surrender all to You. In Jesus mighty name I pray. Amen.

Be Aware Of Your Surroundings

ONE DAY MY mom had asked my cousin and I to go to the store to grab her a few things for dinner. The grocery store wasn't a long walk at all, so I didn't mind. I asked my mom if I could get a few snacks to have before dinner. She said yes as long as I got something for my sisters. As we were coming back from the grocery store, we were talking about school and catching up on family business. I enjoyed being able to catch up with my cousin. We didn't get to see each other often, but when we did, we would crack each other up.

We cut through the old neighborhood field which was a regular route for me when coming back from the store. We were enjoying each other's company when we heard someone yelling.

"Hey! Hey you!" A distant voice said.

We looked around trying to figure out where the

voice was coming from and who they were speaking to. It took us a minute until we realized it was some guy halfway across the field, in a van, trying to get our attention.

"Yea, you, with the light blue jeans. I know y'all hear me." He yells again to assure us he's addressing us.

"No, thank you!" I yelled back hoping he would leave us alone, as I was the one with the light blue jeans. His car door slams. I could hear the rhythmic pace of his steps getting quicker; His footsteps sounded close. So, I ran and without saying a word, my cousin followed. No questions asked. That was our thing, 'if you run, I'm going to run, too!'

"Oh, so y'all do here me," He yelled. "Wait, I just want to get to know y'all!"

We ran like our lives depended on it because it did. The man was chasing us through the field. Thank God we had a head start on him. We ran out of the field, across the street and didn't stop for about two blocks until we were confident that we were safe. We took a moment to gather our breath, as well as our thoughts. We could've been kidnapped. There is no telling what that man had planned to do to us. We knew that the field was near a half-way house, but we never had any problems before.

We made a deal not to tell my mom because she would flip out and put the whole house on lockdown. We just decided not to cut through the field anymore. Thank God we escaped untouched and groceries intact.

Now when guys try to talk to me, I'm mindful of my tone because I don't want another incident like before to happen again. Frankly, no one likes rejection. The spirit of rejection is a powerful spirit that programs you to think and act in a certain manner. Even though you can feel like rejection is part of your life, and it can also feel like it is part of your identity, you have to know that rejection is not you.

A person will feel like they are never good enough when dealing with rejection. Rejection can be tied in with insecurity and even pride. And when someone who deals with the spirit rejection, feels as if they have been rejected, they can do some things outside of their character.

Perhaps at some point in your life, you might be in a situation in which you need to flee for your safety. Here are four things you can do to prevent being in dangerous situations:

1. Be aware of your surroundings. If you were to observe how many people are on their phones texting or on social media while walking, you would discover that it's a lot. If you're on your phone while walking, then your head is down. You're looking at your phone and not those around you. Be aware of people, potential hazards and exits. You never know what can happen, but by being conscious and alert, you might be able to avoid dangerous situations.

2. Trust your instinct. If something doesn't feel right, then go the other way. Perhaps there are some guys

in your pathway that look suspicious or a guy who keeps staring at you while you're out with friends. Is there a car that appears to be following you on your way home? If it doesn't feel right, turn around, cross the street, leave, or do whatever it is you need to do to get yourself in a safe place.

3. If all possible, try to run away. Escape danger and run to safety. It's not cowardly to run away; it's smart and courageous! Your life is precious and valuable, so protect it at all cost.

4. Make a lot of noise. Use noise as a way to attract attention to the situation and get the necessary help. Shout, yell, or scream! Perhaps it will scare your attacker away or at least draw someone's attention. Being quiet and submissive doesn't help the situation. Here is a prayer you can use to pray for protection.

Heavenly Father,

I thank You that You know all and see all. I am grateful that You are mindful of me. Whenever I am in trouble, You are my hiding place, and under Your divine protection is where I can always find refuge. Place Your angels in strategic places, ready to move on my behalf. Lord, lead me away from temptation and help me to be continually aware of the enemy's efforts to distract, deceive, or discourage me. God protect me from danger wherever I go and keep evil far from me The angel of the Lord encamps around those who fear him, and he delivers them (Psalms 34:7). Your goodness and mercy surround me daily, so I will not fear whatever might come against me. In Jesus Mighty name I pray. Amen.

Authentically You

PEER PRESSURE IS something we all encounter, and it comes in different ways. One day in class, my eighth-grade teacher told us to be quiet. I saw that some of the popular kids were upset that we couldn't talk. Not thinking my teacher would hear me across the room but just loud enough for my classmates to hear me, I called the teacher out of her name underneath my breath, but she heard me. That would have worked for another student, but I guess not for me. Just my luck, we had a phone in our classroom that sat on the teacher's desk. My teacher made me call my mom, and she talked to her. I stood there in front of the entire class trying to figure out what my mother was saying. There were some girls laughing at me. I was embarrassed. After my teacher hung up, she informed me to report back to my seat. For the rest of the day, all I could do was focus on the clock. It seemed like time was going by so fast. I hoped that time would slow down because my heart was racing, and I could only imagine what my mother had in store for me.

I knew my mother didn't like for us to act up, especially not in school. My mother would tell us that we were a representation of her and that we must always be on our best behavior. That walk home I couldn't breathe. I think I had a panic attack. When I got home, my mom called me in her room. She asked me what my problem was today, and that she didn't raise me to be like that. She told me that I'm not a follower and that I can't do what everyone else is doing. I'm better than that.

Just as I figured, she whooped me. It hurt my feelings but not as much as my backside. Even though I didn't like getting a whooping, I understood that I shouldn't have been so disrespectful to an adult. After that, I stayed to myself. So much for trying to fit in and be like everyone else.

There was another experience later on that year I wouldn't forget. I was on my way home when I saw my friend hanging behind a building. She caught my attention because I heard her coughing a mile away. I went over to check on her to make sure she was ok.

"Hey Rita, you want to try?" She asked.

"Try what?"

"This cigarette. Try it. This is what everyone is doing. Don't be a lame." She said as she inhaled another puff but with less coughing this time.

I took the cigarette from her hand and imagined how cool I would look. You would see all the pretty women smoking one in the movies, so I guess I would be pretty and cool just like them. I ignored the smell as I laid it on my lip. I took my first puff, and it felt as if my lungs were on fire. It felt as if I was dying. I coughed so hard that I dropped the cigarette on the ground.

"Gross," I yelled. "How can you smoke that? That taste horrible!"

"Hey, you got to do what you got to do to fit in." She said as she bent down to get the cigarette.

I walked away that day disappointed in myself. I knew better, but I gave in to peer pressure. I wanted to be cool so bad that I lost myself and put aside what I knew was right. My mom did tell us that bad company corrupts good character. One of her favorite sayings is "if everyone jumped off the bridge, would you?" I knew I couldn't hang out with her anymore because I wasn't a smoker, nor did I plan on being one.

No matter how many times I failed or was disappointed in myself, I knew that if I was still alive, I had time to become better. Titus 3:3-7 talks about how God redeems us from our foolish and disobedient ways. I walked away that day knowing that what I did was foolish, but I wouldn't do it again.

I begin thinking about what she said, "smoking is what everyone else is doing." I thought about how the cools girls were also having sex. I knew of one girl, in my class that wanted to have sex because everyone else was doing it. Some of the girls were talking about having sex as they were getting dressed in the locker room from PE class. The girl looked at me and said it might as well be my turn. Her comment made me so uncomfortable that I dressed quickly and left. I didn't want to have sex, just because everyone else was doing it.

Trying to be someone else to fit in with others does me no good. Why try to be someone else when I am perfect at being me? They may not like me for who I am but neither will I if I try to be someone else. I know it can be hard trying to fit in with people at school. You want to be liked. You want to be accepted. You want to be understood. Trying to be liked when you're pretending to be someone else hurts you in the long run. You'll lose your true self in trying to keep up with the fake you.

There was a young girl that came in the middle of the school year, and all the girls were picking on her. I knew what it was like being in her shoes, so I became cool with her. She thanked me for being her friend. She was sad because she had personal issues at home and dealing with people not liking her in school made it worse. It's important to be nice to people because you never know what they may be going through.

Sometimes being authentically you is easier said than done. We are constantly bombarded with how good we aren't, how we should look, what others are doing and everything else. We can lose ourselves with everything being thrown at us. To keep up with everything we see and hear we change who we are to fit into everyone else's mold. We got to realize that we were born alone. Everyone has a unique journey. It's not meant for you to fit in. It is my goal to help you break that mold and start living you authentically.

Here are four tips on how to be authentically you;

1. Notice how you feel about yourself around others. Does it make you feel bad or unimportant when you get around people you admire? If so, realize that you are just as important as them. No one has the power to make you feel less than unless you allow them to. Take a step back and acknowledge how you feel and then say "I'm worthy. I'm important. I'm valuable."

2. Journal your feelings. It's important to take note of how you're feeling and when you're feeling it. We have patterns and sometimes to stop those negative feelings we need to know our pattern. Perhaps you act differently when certain people are around. Who are those people?

3. Maintain your values and morals. It can be tempting to do things you usually wouldn't do to fit in but don't. If someone is asking you to do something that conflicts with your values or morals then politely decline. The only person that will hurt in the end is you. You will disappoint yourself. Take and stance by maintaining your standards.

4. Selah. Selah is mentioned 74 times in the bible, and it means to pause and reflect on what has been said. Sometimes it's a matter of taking time to pause and reflect on what God has said about us. God speaks to us and even through his word. John 15:15 says that you are a friend of Jesus. Romans 3:24 states that you have been justified and redeemed. Romans 8:17 states that as a child of God, you are a fellow

heir with Christ. The Bible tells us constantly how God treasures us. Read the Bible and then Selah.

It's easy to get caught up in the hype and begin comparing ourselves to others. Theodore Roosevelt once said "comparison is the thief of joy." My prayer for you is that you learn to love who you are and not compare yourself to others. God didn't create us to fit in but to stand out, and I encourage you to embrace standing out.

HEAVENLY FATHER,

I thank You that I am fearfully and wonderfully made (Psalms 139:14). I thank You that I was created in Your image (Genesis 1:27) and that You love me so much that You have given me a future and hope (Jeremiah 29:11-13). God help me not to compare myself to others and to value what You have placed inside of me. I am loved (John 3:16), and You know my heart (1 Samuel 16:7). When negative thoughts consume me, assure me of my worth and peace that You are with me (Isiah 41:10). When things get hectic, and I lose sight of who I am in You, help me to pause and reflect upon what You have called me. Help me to know my worth as we are all uniquely made. What You have for me, is for me! Let me walk boldly knowing that I am of royalty because I am a child of God. Open my eyes God so that I can see me how You see me. Thank You for loving me, even when I don't love myself. In Jesus mighty name I pray. Amen.

The Beginning Of Something New

MY FRESHMAN YEAR I continued to go to church periodically with my sister. My spirit was being fed, and I was enjoying it increasingly each time I went. I had prayed to God for friendship, more so a brotherly role. I only had sisters, and I always wondered what it felt like to have a big brother. Ashley and I were still cool, but she went to a different high school than me. I would still hang out with her on some weekends. I wanted someone that understood me and someone that I could hang out with at school. God answered my prayers through Anthony. Anthony and I clicked from day one. The first time I met Anthony was in Computer Science. He sat behind me in class. The teacher was explaining something that I didn't fully understand. I put my pencil down and shook my head in frustration. Anthony said something that made me laugh and the rest was history.

Because of all the drama I went through, I was very selective of who I hung out with. Anthony and I became close and stayed inseparable. We even were coined as the "Lame Crew," but I didn't care. I was happy. He always told jokes to make me laugh. He would even walk me home from school and sit on the front porch with me. My mom didn't allow us to have male company because we were still young which was understandable. I didn't complain, and neither did Anthony.

Anthony stayed down the street from Ashley so some weekends we would all hang out together. I would ride the bus to Ashley's, and Anthony would walk over to Ashley's place. We hung out laughing, playing games, talking and just living it up. Normally, I'm quiet around people, but with them, I couldn't stop running my mouth.

As long as I was home by 8:30 PM my mother was ok with me hanging out. She always said I was the responsible one. I was quiet and stayed out of trouble. My mother didn't have to worry about me.

Freshman year was a good year for me and the 'Lame Crew.' I saw Mariah, my childhood friend, often but we didn't do too much talking because we didn't have classes together. My sophomore year was something different. I had developed, and my curvy figure drew attention. Perhaps the wrong attention. One day I was hanging out in the hallway when a guy named Steve rushed up behind me and said I had slept with, Mike, a guy in my class. "No, I didn't!" I yelled, but it didn't matter. He kept walking and laughing, while I was furious. I kept thinking about it all day long. Why do people feel as if it's ok to lie on me?

After school that day, I saw Mike and Steve, outside.

"A, ahhh. Come here!" Yells Steve. He nods his head and proceeds over.

"Yeah, what's up?" Mike said so calmly.

"Hey man, didn't you say you hit that?" Steve loudly announces to get my attention as he pointed to me. I turned around and gave him a quick jab to his shoulder.

"Yeah, I did," Mike said with confidence.

"You're a liar!" I yelled.

"Swear on your grandmamma!" Steve dared him.

"Man, I swear on my grandmother," Mike says definitely.

"Rita, you see he swore on his grandmamma. Soooo-"

"So what? I'm not lying! We didn't sleep together." I assured him.

"Swear on your grandmamma then." Said Steve.

"I swear on my grandmamma," I said with my hand on my hip. I was tired of being lied on. I didn't understand why. All these lies put me in the mindset of not wanting to mess with anyone. This was the seed that led to my trust issues. I no longer desired to be in a relationship at the time. I was disgusted with guys and their need to lie. From that experience, I've gotten stronger and know that people lie to make themselves feel better. I wasn't as bothered as compared to 5th grade. I realized that what I went through in fifth grade made me so much stronger. It gave me tougher skin.

I told Anthony and Ashley what had happened. They uplifted me and at the end had me laughing about everything.

I was embarrassed and felt shame that someone would lie on me about that. *Why would someone say such things about me? What did people think about me?* I was glad I was able to talk to them about it because they made me feel better.

Proverbs 27:9- A sweet friendship refreshes the soul. It's important to have great friends to surround you and keep you uplifted. You are the company you keep. It was a blessing to have Anthony and Ashley in my life. I was happy to be around them and grateful to have them in my life.

Here are three reasons friendship is essential;

1. Support and encouragement. Friends will be there to help you in your lowest moments. When you have a rough patch in life, they are there to make the transition easier. Friends get you even when others don't. They understand you and don't judge you. It doesn't matter if you're a part of the 'cool' group or the 'lame' group. Even though being lame means that you are different, being different is good. Sometimes trying to fit in with people that aren't genuinely your friends will get you in trouble. You may find yourself doing things that you normally wouldn't do just to be accepted. There will be times

that people will lie on you just because they are mean spirited. You know that you aren't what people say about you even though it may hurt. Be confident in yourself but know that your friends will be there to support you through that rough time. They will console you through your hurt. Be true to yourself and the friends will follow.

2. Friends improve the quality of our lives. When we spend time with friends, our hearts are full of joy, laughter, and memories. When you go through hard times, your friends help you bring things into perspective. They bring you advice and words of encouragement that can help carry you through the rough patch. When we have friendships that are full of positivity, our eyes are open to being grateful for genuine people in our life.

3. Acceptance. With sincere friendship, your friends accept you for who you are and not what you can do for them. They know your weaknesses, your flaws, the ugly truth and more, but yet they still love you. They always want the best for you and to see you win.

Below is a prayer on how to choose the right friends for you. As you pray, remember Proverbs 12:26 "The righteous choose their friends carefully, but the way of the wicked leads them astray." Be careful of the friends you have around you. Don't pick your friends off of popularity or wealth.

DEAR GOD,

I thank You for the people You have in my life that provide a comforting arm, a listening ear a shoulder to cry on and even good advice. You have commanded us to love each other in the same way You love us (John 15:12). Lord, help me to be selfless and generous of my time and support for my friends. Friendship is a blessing from God. Please bless my friendships and keep them continuously growing in grace. May our friendships always produce the fruit of the spirit and be a reflection of God's love for us. In Jesus mighty name I pray. Amen.

God's Protection

A MONTH BEFORE MY sophomore year was about to begin, my older cousin asked me to walk with her to see her guy. We were walking down the street when I heard this girl on her front porch say that she didn't like me. I didn't know her, so I paid her no attention and kept walking with my cousin. A few days later my cousin and I were back in the neighborhood visiting a friend of hers. We were in the house chilling for a while when her friend stepped outside knowing it was a group of girls outside waiting for me. When she came back in, she said she was tired and was going to bed. So as soon as my cousin and I walked out of the door, we saw a huge crowd. So, as we walked past the crowd, a girl asked me if I had said something about her. I didn't know her, so I told her no and kept it moving. I turned around to walk off, but she didn't like that because she grabbed my hair from the back and slung me to the ground.

The next thing I knew it was about fifteen girls that

came out of nowhere and jumped me. All I could do was curl up and protect myself. I didn't understand why I was being jumped on. On top of that, I wondered had these girls been following me and plotting against me this entire time. The beating didn't last that long. My cousin and some guys were trying to break up the fight. I heard one of the girls' yell 'let's go,' and they all took off running. I laid on the ground for a few seconds and got up as soon as they left. More emotionally hurt than physically because I got up with no scratches. I knew it was God protecting me. Fifteen against one and nothing was broken or bruised. That was all God. Afterwards, I went home. I prayed and asked God, why do these things keep happening to me? *Why do people find it necessary to pick on me and cause trouble with me?*

After that incident, I found out that the girl that started the fight attended my school. She and her friends would come by my division and pick on me, threatening to fight me. When I discovered that we had the same lunch period, I would sit in the restroom or avoid lunch altogether.

When school let out, I would wait and walk the long way home because she was always with a group of girls and I didn't want another incident to happen. It wasn't too long afterwards that I found out that they had jumped another girl and had put her in the hospital. After weeks of hiding, I discovered the reason why she jumped me was because the guy she liked, liked me.

God protects us in so many ways. Below you will find the various ways that God protect us;

1. He speaks to us. John 10:27 (NIV)- "My sheep listen to my voice; I know them, and they follow me."

   God speaks to us, but we have to be able to listen to Him and follow His instructions. The instructions He gives can save your life. It's important that we have a relationship with Christ, so we don't miss out when He speaks to us.

2. Protecting us from danger seen and unseen. Proverbs 3:26 (NIV)- "…for the LORD WILL BE AT YOUR SIDE and will keep your foot from being snared." There are so many things that can happen to us every day, but we may never know them all because God kept them from happening to us. We should wake up every day thanking God for his divine protection.

3. Using willing people. Ephesians 4:2 (NIV) – "Be completely humble and gentle; be patient, bearing with one another in love." God uses people around us to help us – the nurse who gives us medicine, your grandparents who give you wise counseling, or the teacher that supplies you with the knowledge you need- God uses people every day. God can use people to give you advice to keep you from harm's way. When your mother tells you to stay away from a certain crowd, listen. When your teachers tell you to take your education seriously, focus. God protects us by using everyday people that are willing to help.

   Below is a prayer on how to trust God when you're going through a rough patch. Keep John 15:16-19

(NIV) in mind which states, "I no longer call you servants, because a servant does not know His master's business. Instead, I have called you friend, for everything I learned from my Father I have made known to you. You did not choose me, but I chose you and appointed you so that you might go and bear fruit—fruit that will last—and so that whatever you ask in my name the Father will give you. This is my command: Love each other. 'If the world hates you, keep in mind that it hated me first. If you belonged to the world, it would love you as its own. As it is, you do not belong to the world, but I have chosen you out of the world. That is why the world hates you." God calls us his friends, and because the world doesn't like God, the world doesn't like us. This scripture was the answer to why I was going through everything I went through. Made me realize that some people see the light in you. Even though you may not see it, there's something special about you.

DEAR GOD,

I thank You for Your divine protection from dangers seen and unseen. I thank You for having your angels to keep watch over me. Deuteronomy 31:6 (NIV) reminds me to "be strong and courageous. Do not be afraid or terrified because of them, for the LORD your God goes with you; he will never leave you nor forsake you." I know that our struggle is not against flesh and blood, but against the rulers, against the powers, against the world forces of this darkness, against the spiritual forces of wickedness in the high places. Dress me in the armor of God so that I can stand firm against the schemes of the enemy. Help me Lord to trust You as my refuge and strength. God, You are faithful, and You will strengthen and protect me from the evil one according to 2 Thessalonians 3:3. I pray You will make me strong and courageous in the presence of danger, recognizing that You have overcome and will set right all injustice and wrong one day. Help me not to be resentful, hateful or bitter towards those that try to harm me. Help me have a heart full of love and see them how You see them, God. I know that there is no love, greater than Christ's love. God help me to embody that type of love towards all. In Jesus mighty name I pray. Amen.

Betrayal

MY JUNIOR YEAR in high school, I became close with a girl name Tina. We had a few classes together so over time we bonded over how crazy our teachers were. We would hang out after school having girl talk. On the weekends, when we had a few dollars, we would go out to eat. She understood me, so it was easy to talk to her. I confided in her about personal issues. The guys that liked me, how hard it was trying to fit in and just life. She made me feel comfortable being myself around her.

After years of insecurity and people overlooking me, I was coming into my own. My relationship with God was getting stronger. Even though I wasn't popular, I was starting to feel confident in myself. On top of all of that, I had a genuine friendship, I thought.

But after some time I noticed that Tina started acting differently. She would begin to say smart remarks about the way I look, trying to tear me down. She would say that I looked cute… for a dark-skinned girl. She flirted with the guys that liked me, behind my back. When I asked her about it, she denied it. It didn't bother me that she was talking to these guys, but I felt she was targeting them specifically. The situation became worse, it was like she was trying to be me. She started talking about me in front of my face. Like hello! She was in competition with me, to be me. She wanted my life but didn't know half of the things I had been through.

I didn't understand how someone could be your friend one day and then the next they are your arch nemesis. I didn't hate her. I was just hurt because she broke my trust. Some people can dislike you, and you'll never know the real reason. She was insecure in who she was. Instead of being a friend and confiding about how she felt, she turned those feeling into hurtful words towards me.

I was ignoring all the signs until finally I got fed up. No matter how long you've been friends with a person when God says it's time to let go, that means to let it go. Even though we don't see why we should end a friendship, God does. He knows what's best for us.

The enemy was using her to plant a seed of low self-esteem in me. I refused to go back to the person I use to be.

We see people from the outside, but God sees the inside. We know what they tell us but God knows their motive. When you pray and ask God for signs follow them. The answer may not be what you want to hear, but if you take heed to the instructions, then it will put you in the direction you need to go.

Friendship is special. It grows, matures, and stretches us. Friendship plays a role in determining our sense of self and the direction of our lives. When you have a genuine friendship where both parties want the best for each other, it is how God intended it.

True friendships require you to be vulnerable and honest with each other. It may be uncomfortable to talk about certain stuff, such as if you are jealous of your friend, but it's needed. No one is perfect, and I'm sure a true friend will let you know how beautiful you are inside and out. Listen to a person long enough; and they will begin to show their true colors. God gave me so many signs, but I kept ignoring them until I got fed up. Here are three tips for having a genuine friendship;

1. There should be no competition. Friendship isn't about who's better but how you two can grow together. Be willing to serve and be there for each other. Not tear the other person down. It benefits no one. You may think tearing the other person down will make you feel better, but it doesn't.

2. Have a common purpose or something that bonds you. Friendship isn't based on someone who keeps your secrets but someone who you share a common purpose with. It can be that you two want to be better people as you mature, you want the best for each other, you both have a relationship with Christ, or you both have an interest in building a genuine

friendship. There needs to be a common purpose so that when the friendships come to a rough patch, you can think back on why you two became friends (Proverbs 22:24-25).

3. Pray for each other. You should be able to pray for your friends and want to see their relationship with God deepened. This is an act of selflessness. Pray for discernment.

As you prepare your heart for prayer, think of this scripture, "There is no greater way to love than to give your life for your friends (John 15:13)."

DEAR GOD,

I know that friendship is a gift You have given us. Lord, surround me with people who genuinely want me to succeed, and I desire the same for them. Lord let it not be a competition amongst us, but a desire for us to grow in You. Let us exemplify Christ's love as He did with Judas. Lord guide me in the right direction and give me the strength to separate from those who do not have my best interest at heart. Let me trust You fully. Let me show myself friendly and speak kind words unto others. Let me be confident in myself, so I may never have the desire to tear down another. In Jesus' mighty name I pray. Amen.

Looking For Love In All The Wrong Places

MY SENIOR YEAR in high school, I was longing for a relationship. I saw everyone else in a relationship, and I wanted one too. I was looking for love when I didn't even truly love myself. I felt like being in a relationship would provide me the validation that I was loveable. I lucked up and ended up in a relationship with a guy, named Marcus, that went to my school. I was so excited when he asked me out. I was getting what I wanted. Thank you, God!

My head was so up in the clouds and my feelings so caught up in 'love' that I was blind to what was happening. At first, I dismissed his slightly shallow comments because I didn't know my worth and how I should be treated. I was just happy that someone wanted to be with me. It was a series of incidents that led up to me realizing that this relationship wasn't the best for me.

The first incident was at the beginning of us dating; he started telling me how I should act and what I should and shouldn't do. I listened. I realized he was slowly changing me into the person he wanted me to be. I started seeing him flirt with other girls. Even though they knew we were dating, some would look at me and smirk. He had so much control over me.

He didn't even want me talking to my friends anymore, so I distanced myself from them. I was so mean to everyone because I was hurt by the way he treated me, even though I treated him with the utmost respect. When we went out, he did all the talking. He never wanted to post me on social media. I tried so hard to make him happy, but nothing worked. After all I did for him he still treated me wrong.

The second incident was when my best friend Anthony called and told me he wanted to be honest with me and tell me that Marcus was no good for me. He told me that I deserved better and people were looking at me like I was dumb for talking to him. He said that I shouldn't settle. No matter how bad it hurt, I needed to let go because he was changing me for the worst. When he told me, I didn't pay him any mind. I was in denial.

A few days later, I was walking to class and as I was walking by, I saw him hugging on another girl. We gave each other eye contact, but he pretended as if he didn't see me. He turned his back and began to walk off with the girl. That was the straw that broke the camel's back for me.

I stood there for a minute in disbelief as to what just happened. My disbelief was interrupted as someone bumped me as they were walking by. I gathered my thoughts and headed to class. All day I couldn't do anything but think about what I saw. *Why was he with another girl? Why did he pretend as if he didn't see me? What the heck was going on?* Unfortunately, we didn't see each other for the remainder of the day. I even waited after school in the usual spot we would meet, but he didn't show.

I walked home angry. I wanted answers.

When I got home, I went to my room and sulked. It's was about an hour later when the phone rang. My sisters weren't around, and my mom was at work.

"Hello," I answered.

"Hi, is Rita home?" It was Marcus.

"What Marcus?" I asked.

"Babe-"

"Babe? Oh, so you know me now?" I interrupted.

"It's not like that. You know I got my image to protect. I'm known for being with a certain type of girl."

"Your image! What does that have to do with me? Aren't we in a relationship?" At that very moment, Anthony's words came to mind, that I deserve better and that I shouldn't settle.

"Hold up! Better yet, we're no longer in a relationship!" I assured him.

"What!?! You know no one else is gonna want you and treat you how I treat you. " He threatened.

"There's always someone better!"

"Yea, right. We will see. You ain't gonna find nobody better than me."

I left that conversation feeling worthless. I reflected on previous discussions and noticed how he made me feel as if he was the only one that wanted me and I couldn't do better. He verbally abused me, and I allowed it because my self-esteem was low. Within a week time frame of our last conversation, I discovered that I wasn't the only girl he was dating. I was tired of being treated like crap, so I'm glad I ended the relationship. I wanted to be in a relationship but not at the expense of being stepped on. As I stated, I was looking for love when I didn't even love myself. We can get so caught up in trying to figure out what others like about us when in reality the best thing is to figure yourself out and find love and happiness within self — not man.

It's ok to want to be loved. When you realize that God loves you, you'll feel so much better. You won't want to tolerate any mess. Know that you're supposed to be treated like the Queen you are and never settle for less.

It's best to get to know yourself first so that no man can change you.

Unhealthy relationships can take a toll on you and your self-worth. Don't settle and feel as if you have to stay in a relationship in which you aren't wanted. If you feel as if your relationship is turning for the worse or you're getting concerned, then please tell a trusted source such as a parent or a counselor. Understand that the love a man gives can't even come close to the love that God gives you. God's love is unconditional, and He will never let you down. Here are four signs you're in an unhealthy relationship;

1. Verbal abuse is when someone uses their words to manipulate you and,or control you through shaming you or talking down to you. This is also a form of emotional abuse. No one should try to make you feel bad about yourself, manipulate you, or attack your self-worth. If you're in a verbally abusive relationship, tell a trusted source and get out of the relationship.

2. Physical abuse is when someone puts their hands on you. It can be when someone slaps you, kicks you, punches you, or even shoves you. When physical abuse first happens, some people dismiss it as a onetime thing, but it's rarely a onetime incident. When your relationship becomes physically abusive, get out as soon as you can. Call the National Domestic Violence Hotline; their advocates are available 24/7 at 1-800-799-SAFE (7233) in over 200 languages. All calls are free and confidential.

3. Cheating on you intentionally is another sign you're in an unhealthy relationship. No one wants to be cheated on, and no one deserves it. If your partner is displaying signs of acting jealous, possessive or

accusing you of being with other partners, then it's a possibility that your partner is insecure. Talk to your partner about why they would feel this way.

4. In today's time, social media, your phone, and the Internet can be mediums for people to abuse you. If someone is sending you insulting or threatening messages over text, email or social media or looking through your phone, then this is a form of digital abuse. Always remember that love doesn't hurt.

Ignore those that don't appreciate you. Surround yourself with people that are positive. No one has the right to make you feel bad about yourself. Don't let people's negative comments get you down. So avoid anyone that brings you down.

Dear God,

Thank You for Your unconditional love towards me and thank You for sending Your only begotten Son, Jesus Christ to die on the cross for my sins. There is no greater love (John 15:13). Fulfill me with the love of Christ that I may love others in the same way that Christ loves me. Help me love myself and to know my worth. Let me not be consumed with looking for love in all the wrong places but let me experience more of Your love (Jeremiah 31:3).

Give me discernment so I may know those that mean me harm and the strength to forgive those that have hurt me. Let me take every negative thought and feeling I have for them and create in me a clean heart that will love them how You love them, see them how You see them and speak to them, how You would speak to them. In Jesus mighty name I pray. Amen.

Loving The Skin You Are In

MONTHS LATER AFTER my breakup, I pushed myself to start focusing more on school, but I was still hurt. I looked at myself in the mirror. I was disgusted with myself and started saying how ugly I was. People treated me the way they did because I thought I was ugly. *Would people treat me better if I was lighter?* I listened to all the rap songs as they talked about how light skinned girls were what every man wanted. It just made me dislike everything about myself more. I wanted to be what every man wanted. I want to be that girl they were rapping about.

All my life people have been cruel to me. Because of my gums and lips being so dark, people constantly asked me if I smoked cigarettes. So, I hated smiling. I started looking and comparing myself with other girls on social media, and the music videos wishing I looked the way they did to please a man.

I realized that I only wanted to date light skin guys because if I had a child, I wouldn't want them going through the same things I went through. I just thought dark was ugly, in general, from the things I had experienced.

So, I searched online on how to make my skin lighter. I ordered some products, and in a couple of days, it came in the mail. I used the product over and over. My skin was getting lighter. No one noticed what I had done. But I still felt the same on the inside. Two weeks passed, and I walked to my cousin's house. He looked at me and started laughing asking why did I bleach my skin. He told me that I was beautiful just the way God made me and to stop using that cream. So, I went home, stared at myself in the mirror and cried. I began apologizing to God telling Him that He didn't make any mistakes when He created me. Luckily it was spring, so the sun was shining abundantly. I stop using the cream, and my skin went back to normal within weeks. From that day I realized that I was beautiful inside and out.

After what I did, I talked to my mom telling her about the mistake I made. She told me that people use to tell her that she was the prettiest out of her siblings, simply because she was the lightest. She didn't know why people thought that, but she's noticed that over the years too many people didn't like being dark skinned because of the history behind it. We talked a little and my mom encouraged me and gave me words of wisdom.

After our conversation, I realized that it's best to get to know yourself first and the way that God created you so that you won't go by social media and let others define you.

God made no mistakes with any of us. If a person doesn't like you because of your looks, that's fine. It just means that it wasn't meant for them to be a part of your life. God will send the right people in your life if you pray and ask Him to. Don't get discouraged when you ask God to bring the right people in your life, and people leave. He's making room for the people He wants in your life. People who will stay with you through it all. It's ok if people don't see your worth. God says that you are worthy! Here are three tips on how to love the skin you're in;

1. Remember you're the only one there is. You're unique. No one can be like you. Celebrate and own your uniqueness.

2. Focus on the things you like about yourself. We focus on the negative so much that it consumes all our thoughts. We magnify the negative but what will happen when we focus on the positive and magnify that instead. You will have a more positive attitude about yourself. When you feel positive about yourself, it increases your confidence.

3. Open up and talk. Talking about how you feel can help. Perhaps you'll realize that everyone has something about themselves that they don't like and that you're not alone.

Dear God,

When I look in the mirror, I don't like what I see. I see the darkness of my skin tone, the shape of my body, and the blemishes on my skin. Help me not to focus on my flaws but to love myself as You love me. According to Proverbs 3: 3-4 help me to clothe myself in love and faithfulness, let me love every inch of me, inside and out. Jesus, You paid the price of the lack of my perfection. Help me to break free from the bondage of striving for perfection and find the beauty of who I am. Let me be at peace with my body and not envy others. Give me strength when I want to hide. Help me to see my life through Your eyes. In Jesus' mighty name I pray. Amen

Never Let Your Past Hold You Down

WE'VE ALL GONE through different things in life like; molestation, abandonment, identity crisis, etc. We don't have the answers as to why we go through these things. As a result of what we've been through, we can feel as if we aren't worthy. Worthy of being loved, worthy of respect, worthy of financial freedom, worthy of God's grace and mercy. But know that's not the case. God's intentions were for us to overcome these obstacles and not let them keep us down. He wanted us to come out stronger, not broken.

I believe when we go through trials and tribulations in life, they were meant to happen; not only to make us stronger but to help someone else overcome what might have broken them completely. Don't be ashamed; just know you are not alone. Not saying it will be easy as it's an overnight process to let go but if you hold on to it not only is it emotionally draining but it also takes up so much time. As we know, time is precious, and we can't get it back.

The enemy tries to keep bringing up your past because he knows that God has something great in store for you in your future. The beauty about life is that we don't know what the future may hold in store for us, but that's where faith comes in. So don't continue to look back. Sometimes we worry about the future but as it states in Matthew 6:31-34. "So do not worry, saying, 'What shall we eat?' or 'What shall we drink?' or 'What shall we wear?' For the pagans run after all these things, and your heavenly Father knows that you need them. But seek first His kingdom and His righteousness, and all these things will be given to you as well. Therefore, do not worry about tomorrow, for tomorrow will worry about itself. Each day has enough trouble of its own."

Don't let your past determine your future. You aren't what you use to be; you're in transition, so stop holding on to your past. Don't allow others to hold you to your past either. Even when people bring up what you use to do or how you use to be, shake it off. Let them know that was the old you. If they don't believe you, then 'oh well.' Keep moving. Sometimes it can take a while before people see the change in you because they are so used to the old you. I've learned in life that we have to forgive ourselves first and foremost.

Forgiving others is easier said than done, but for you to get peace, you have to push yourself. Some of us are battling a lot of demons in life because of some of the things we did in the past. In the Bible, it says, "forgive so we can be forgiven." God genuinely loves us, and we must let all the dead weight we carry go. No matter how many times it comes to your head just know you are forgiven. Let go!

You will be tested to see if the change you say you have made is true. Honestly, you might not pass the first time around, or the third, but keep trying. Every day is a new day. Each opportunity is a chance to get it right. If God is still waking you up every day, you can always start over.

A friend once told me that it's not about the fall you take it's about the comeback you make. Remember, you got this. So when temptation comes around, hold onto 1 Corinthians 10:13 in which God will make a way out of escape. No temptation is too great for you. God does not give you more than you can handle. He will make a way of escape, but you have to want it. When that old boyfriend pops back up, God has made a way of escape. You have to take it. When that urge to make money in the streets comes over you, God has made a way of escape. You have to want it. When you feel peer pressure to take drugs, God has made a way of escape. Listen to God and not them.

Trying to outrun your past can be tiring. But who said you have to run from it? Everyone has skeletons in their closets. It's just that some of us hid them better than others. Learn from your past and not hold onto any regrets. Release them. Sometimes we question God about the people in our lives. They may have been there for a reason. Whatever that reason may have been; it was for your benefit. Here are three things you can do to break free from the past;

1. Pray. Pray to God to heal you and break free from any bondage of the past. Ask Him to deliver you from things that are not for you. God is a god that can heal, deliver and set free. When you are broken, He can make you whole.

2. Look in the mirror and tell yourself you're not your past. It takes time to build up your confidence to know that you are a new creature in Christ and not your old self. In building yourself back up, you need encouragement. What better person to encourage you than yourself? Look at yourself in the mirror and say "I am not my past! My past does not determine my future! I am a new creature in Christ! Begin to say this daily until you believe it. It will feel uncomfortable at first, but it's needed.

   Stop fearing what people will think of your past. God loves you in spite of, and for those that genuinely love you, they will do the same. You can't find yourself through man that can only be done through God. You can't hide anything from God. He knew us in our mother's womb (Jeremiah 1:5). He even knows how many hairs we have on our heads (Matthew 10:30-31). Have faith and know deep down inside that He forgave you and that's all that truly matters.

   So many of us have so many scars deep within us

that haven't healed because we haven't let go of the things that hurt us. You need to know and believe that you are not your past and you're worthy of good happening to you. Please be encouraged. God will restore you if you truly let Him in. He will comfort you. God will get you through the storm, and everything that you've gone through you will look back at it and laugh.

3. Forgive others and yourself. Forgive those that have hurt you, including yourself. Forgiving others allows you to move past the hurt. Forgiving someone means that you've made peace with the pain and you are ready to let it go. You don't want to stay in that old state of mind. When you forgive someone, it's not for them. It's for you. By not forgiving someone you hold yourself in the bondage of bitterness and brokenness. By forgiving them, you move closer to being whole. When forgiving others, a lot of the times, we forget to forgive ourselves.

How does one forgive themselves? Accept that you aren't perfect and have made some mistakes. Know that you are not the mistakes that you have made and that you are even better because of the mistakes. God knew that we were going to make mistakes in life. In the midst of it all, He still loves us all the same. Just remember He chastise the ones He loves. Never think once that life will be perfect and that you don't have to go through battles. The only way you'll grow is if you go through things and learn from them.

Don't stay in the wilderness for too long. Meaning don't dwell on your past forever. Some people will never make it out of the wilderness, meaning some people will never move past their past. They will keep themselves captive to what was and never moving forward to what can become. You'll find yourself going through the same thing over and over again until you get it right and when you do, you'll be stronger than ever. Life is like a test to make us stronger, but don't ever think that God is punishing you (Romans 12:12).

You can overcome any and everything with God by your side. He loves us so much. God's intent was never to harm or hurt us. Remember, He won't put you through more than you can bear. Greater is He that is in you than He that is in the world (1 John 4:4). When you read the prayer below, I want you to believe it. I want you to pray it over and over again until you understand the power these words hold. Don't allow your past to win. Once you overcome, you will be able to help others overcome the same thing you've been through. When a person tells you that you're just like someone in your family, in a bad way, don't get upset. Simply pray against it. You don't have to say a word to them. But when you get a chance, pray against all generational curses in your bloodline. Just remember God hears your prayers, and He feels your hurt. It'll be ok. I declare that you are more than a conqueror and you shall slay every Goliath that comes your way. When I'm down and out and feel like everyone is against me, I read Psalms 25.

Never Let Your Past Hold You Down

FATHER GOD,

I come to You as humble as I know how. I ask that You help me to move out of the shadows of my past and help me to see that You have greatness in store for me. My past does not disqualify me but prepares and strengthens me. I am not my mistakes nor the shame of my past. All have sinned and fallen short of Your glory, yet You still love us. You still love me. Lord, help me to see me how You see me and not less than. Lord, help me to know that I am worthy of love and worthy of good things happening to me. I thank You, God, for walking with me daily and helping me recover from my past. I no longer want to be in bondage to my past, so I forgive those that have hurt me, including myself. I no longer want to hold onto this hurt, so I cling to Your peace and healing virtue (Galatians 5:22-23). God, I thank You as I enter into the newness and let go of the past. In Jesus mighty name I pray. Amen.

There Is Beauty In Being Different

BEING DIFFERENT COMES with the territory. You can either stand out and shine with your uniqueness or be stared at with disapproving eyes. Your uniqueness is not a flaw; it is what makes you different from other people. We tend to point out all of our flaws. Things that others don't even see, we see in ourselves. It's said that we are our own worst critics.

Growing up, I always wondered why I didn't fit in or why God made me the way I am. I wondered if it was not by His creation but by my genetics and spirit. Was it possible that God created me different for a unique purpose or saw something in me I had not seen in myself? Too often I would isolate myself in my search to find out why I was on this earth. Why I had to be so different when everyone else seemed so alike? It is okay to feel lonely like you have no one to talk or relate to. Sometimes God needs you to Himself. He makes time to listen to all His children and even answers their prayers when they least expect it. All you have to do is talk to Him through prayer. As long as you have God by your side, not saying things will be easy, but they will be better. Don't get too discouraged. Pray, be still and listen. You are right where God wants you to be.

I realized that I was different because I had the darkest skin color out of all of my sisters. I was teased about my body features. While I despised my abnormal features, I came across a scripture that put me into perspective about my body. The scripture states, "But now, O Lord, you are our Father; we are the clay, and you are our potter; we are all the work of your hand (Isaiah 64:8 ESV)." This meant that everyone is molded differently in the shape that God intended. Now, when I look in the mirror, I realize how much I love my big nose, big eyes, big cheekbones, big feet, small teeth, dark lips, dark gums, and skin complexion too! This is the way God made me, and I love it. You don't have to be a size 2 or 10 to be loved. God loves us all equally.

Back when I was a teenager everyone got teased for wearing glasses or having braces. Now, glasses are trendy, and braces are worn by kids, teens, and young adults. Just remember, trends come and go, and you do not need to jump on every bandwagon.

My mom never dressed me in name brand clothing, but she made sure I was presentable. I thank God for that because now I do the same for my children. You don't have to go broke and spend your last on trying to impress people. I wear the cheapest clothing and still get complimented on my attire.

If I had believed what my bullies teased me about, I would've been a different person. I would have seen my features as flaws by design and not unique attributes. Take this to heart by letting no one define you and remember always to be yourself. No one knows you as you do. Maybe someday your closest friends will share your features, and it will be a positive talking point and bonding experience.

Every day we meet or see new people. On the surface, someone can appear like they have their life together, but behind closed doors, they are hurting. Always treat people with kindness and humbleness. By showing a little bit of kindness to someone, you can brighten their day. God's just building you up for a higher purpose, and we can all share a common purpose by being kind to one another.

Instead of dwelling on the negatives of being different let's focus on the positives.

DEAR GOD,

I thank You that I am uniquely made in Your image and that I am one of a kind. Help me to appreciate and love the way You created me to be. Help me to love every part of me, even the parts that I see as imperfect. Help me to see myself the way You see me. Thank you, God, that I am fearfully and wonderfully made. I thank You, God, that when people talk bad about me that

I won't take it personally and get offended. It's not a reflection of me but themselves. God, You have made us for Your glory and to serve You. Help me not mistreat my body and for me to know that my body is a holy temple for You to dwell in. Knowing that I am unique humbles me, God, because You loved me enough to take your time in making me and see that there was no other person like me. Thank You, God. In Jesus mighty name I pray. Amen.

Don't Give Up On Life. Life's Good Outweighs The Bad.

I REMEMBER ONE NIGHT as I was asleep, the Lord showed me a dream. I was sitting on the floor, with my legs crossed, rocking back and forth. I was concerned and nervous within the dream. Facing my closet crying, I asked the Lord, "Why did I have to go through this?" But before I could asked God another question, a voice said 'Look at how strong you are. It's ok. You've made it!" These words kept repeating over and over again until I woke up.

I woke up in a place of peace and restoration. The dream assured me that I was strong and all I went through served a purpose and that purpose is to help you! You don't have to wait until you are 30 years old to know your worth. You can realize that now.

Self-worth is defined as "the sense of one's value or

worth as a person." Be confident in who you are— your weight, height, skin complexion and everything that makes you. Without a favorable view of one's self, it will be hard to have high self-worth. The more you believe in yourself, the happier you will be in life.

Everyone can possess confidence, and it's essential for you to learn how to find it and own it, flaws and all. You may wonder, how can you build your confidence, when you're already broken or can't find something to be happy about?

First, let's try setting a goal. It can be anything. It can be a hobby, something you're passionate about or something you never dreamed of doing. It can be big or small but set a goal and accomplish it. If it's a big goal, then break it down into smaller steps and give yourself credit as you completed those small steps. As you accomplish your goals, your confidence builds because you will be proud that you've made progress. Keeping busy on your goal frees your mind on thinking of negative thoughts.

Second, fall in love with self. Yes, I said it, fall in love with yourself! Every day I want you to look in the mirror and tell yourself how beautiful, bold, talented, confident and intelligent you are. I want you to say to yourself that there is nothing you can't accomplish. You are strong, you are wise, you are capable, and you are deserving of love!

You have to do this. It may seem weird at first but trust me, it gets better with time. You begin to believe the words that you speak. You start to see yourself as those things you declare, and that's because you are indeed all those things. It's just that your vision got clouded with all the negativity.

Third, what does your body say? Your body language speaks for you, even when you haven't said a word. People can tell if you are insecure by the way you walk, talk, sit and interact with others. You speak softly, your back is slumped over, your head is hung low, your arms are folded, and you have the look of 'leave me alone!'

Let's change that. To build your confidence you have to change your body language. Sit up straight and hold your head up. Unfold your arms and look at whomever you're speaking with. Be approachable even if it's uncomfortable. It's going to be a stretch, but after a while, it will become second nature and people will notice the change in you. Building confidence is a process just like everything else, so even when you have a bad day, don't beat yourself up. Try again the next day!

Confidence does not come from a number on the scale, how many people like you, liked your post, or how many people viewed your video. All of those things create a temporary feeling. Your self-worth is how you think of yourself, so learn to make your thoughts positive.

With all the stuff I've been through; being lied on, my sister's teasing me, my father abandoning me, being abused, jumped on, trying to commit suicide, and having friends betray me, I ought to have lost my mind.

It was by the grace of God and me praying that I made it and you can too. Don't let no one or nothing stop you, no matter how hard life can get. Joy comes in the morning, meaning bad things don't last forever.

Not everyone in your life is out to get you. People do make mistakes and when they do, forgive them. Release all that negativity so you can be free and live your best life. Find happiness within yourself. I can honestly say I found it through Christ. I wish I would've found Him earlier in life, but everything happened for His perfect reason. In the book of Psalms 34: 18-19(NIV) it states "The Lord is close to the brokenhearted and saves those who are crushed in the spirit. The righteous person may have many troubles but the Lord delivers them all." Don't give up!

FATHER GOD,

There are times when I am unsure of who I am, and I search for my value in the world. I lose focus and lose sight of You. Remind me of who I am so that I can walk confidently and assured of Your love for me. "For thou hast possessed my reins; thou hast covered me in my mother's womb. I will praise thee; for I am fearfully and wonderfully made; marvelous are thy works; and that my soul knoweth right well (Psalm 139: 13-14)." When I lose track and begin to think negatively, gently nudge me back. Let me focus on Your grace, mercy and those things that bring me joy. Fill my heart full of love so that I may forgive those that have hurt me. Let me not hold onto any grudges but know that you have called me to love my neighbor as I love myself. Give me the courage to love myself, my family and friends unconditionally. Help me to be better in these areas, and bring you joy. In Jesus mighty name. Amen.

In loving memory of
Anthony Hayes

September 25th, 1987-March 24th, 2015

I THANK GOD for letting us cross paths. I prayed for a brother, and God sent you. Even though you're gone, you have made a great impact in my life. As I always say 13 years of our friendship has passed, but my love for you will always last. You will always and forever be in my heart

Love always

54263432R00065

Made in the USA
Columbia, SC
28 March 2019